ALCOHOLIC BY CHOICE

A SELF-INFLICTED SICKNESS

CAROL B. GRIFFITH

WINEPRESS WP PUBLISHING

ISBN 1-57921-465-7

ACCLAIM FOR
ALCOHOLIC BY CHOICE

—⚬⚬⚬—

In her potent little book, *Alcoholic by Choice,* Carol speaks out against the fallacy of transferring alcoholic addiction to treatment programs and systems! She invites problem drinkers to allow their sobriety to come about as an extension of choosing an intentional, personal relationship with Jesus Christ, the Author and Finisher of all faith and healing. Alcoholics are challenged to accept ownership for their lives, including the choice to drink. Carol writes with the gentle confidence of one who plummeted into the painful rigors of alcoholic hardship and surfaced in sweet victory.

—Sharon Davis, M.S.
Discovery Counseling
Renton, WA 90859

If you are seriously seeking permanent recovery from alcoholism—and open to hearing Truth—this is a must-read book. Carol has been to hell and back. When A.A. and the 12-Step Program proved only a temporary fix, she returned to the bottle again and again. Each time her condition grew worse. It was only through Jesus that she found a lasting solution.

This book pulls no punches. Her hard-hitting comments and substantiating facts will appeal to the honest mind. Is alcoholism a disease or a choice? This book will answer your questions and put you on the path to permanent sobriety.

—Nancy L. Hagerman
Author, *In The Pit*

PROLOGUE

—◦◦◦—

*A*lcoholic by Choice is my story. It is a true record of how God rescued me from the bottle and transformed me into a new person. I have lived a sober and productive life, free of addiction, for twenty-one years as of this writing. The credit for my successful new life is not mine. It is God's.

The helps available to me in the late seventies were Alcoholics Anonymous, secular and Christian counseling, hospitalizations with psychiatric help, and medication. I tried them all. They all failed me.

My focus in this book is based on the idea that drunkenness is sin, not a disease. In my life, freedom from addiction came directly from my belief that God could and would deliver me from *all* my sins.

Alcoholics Anonymous and the 12-Step recovery program became obstacles to my growth, once I placed my life in God's care. My story examines some of the issues I found in conflict with God's Word, the Bible.

I will compare the power of God to rid us of our destructive habits against the weaknesses of science, health care providers, and treatment programs.

I am compelled to write this book for those who struggle with addictions and have found little hope in existing programs. It is my prayer that this book will open doors to the promise of forgiveness, a cure, and a new life in Christ. We do not need to be forever *recovering*. We can be free!

The difference between the teachings in the Bible and that of AA's *Big Book* is fundamentally important. Many recovery programs use the *Big Book* as a primer for recovering. In the early days of AA, the pioneers of the program chose to alter the acknowledgment of God, to speak only of a "higher power," so that no alcoholic would be offended by the name of God.

Additional chapters were added to explain what "spirituality" and "spiritual awakening" meant. In the chapter, "Spiritual Experience," the writers explain it as a "personality change" and an "educational experience." In the first printing of the *Big Book*, many readers got the impression that the personality changes were a sudden and a miraculous religious experience. "Happily for everyone, this conclusion is erroneous," the writer comments (AA, *Big Book*, ALCOHOLIC ANONYMOUS WORLD SERVICES, Inc., New York City, p. 569).

The Bible's Author offers a miracle, an intervention that will transform the heart and life of those who will believe on the name of the Lord Jesus Christ, the Son of God.

I can remember how hard it was to read or even think when sobering up. For that reason, I have kept research statistics on alcoholism to a minimum. It is my wish to write my story as simply as I can. I want the person who picks up this book to be able to grasp the truth of God's great love—love that will not let us go, even in our drunken despair.

Scripture references are primarily from the New King James Version unless otherwise indicated. Words peculiar to Alcoholics Anonymous are italicized, along with other words indicating my thoughts.

CHAPTER ONE

—⟨⟨⟨⟨∞⟩⟩⟩⟩—

An alcoholic is anyone you don't like who drinks more than you do. —Dylan Thomas

Becoming hooked on alcohol was as easy as falling in love. And when I came into the esteemed rooms of Alcoholics Anonymous for help, I believed they had the answer to all my problems. They didn't.

I feared leaving them. If I didn't stay with the *program* I would end up a hopeless drunk, so I was told. Their stories back this up, and it scared me. They had me. It became a relationship of dependence for me. I was stuck with a new partner for life: AA.

My attraction to the alcoholic life began when I was young and wanting all the pleasures I thought I should have. After I graduated from nursing school in a rural town in Pennsylvania, my roommate and I moved to New York to work and find an exciting new life.

One evening we sat in the cabaret listening to Jazz. The black and white keyboard, like a tuxedo of strung-out tiles, suited our pretentious mood. The heightened beat of our hearts brought a rosy flush to our cheeks. Our imaginations burst into flame with recollections of romantic scenes from movies we had seen. Lifting our goblets, we toasted New York for all it promised.

Carol B. Griffith

We stepped from our ordinary lives, our plain clothes, and our unimaginative conversations into glamorous roles. We pretended to be something we had dreamed about, fanned by the winds of youth and inexperience. My roommate and I had just graduated and were bursting with reckless abandon. Our eyes danced around the room looking at the unattached young men. *Is that handsome guy at the bar looking at me?* A quick mental review of my pose, my hair, my dress told me, yes, I look good. I tingled all over. This evening was playing out just like the movies. *Was I drunk or was this moment too intoxicating?*

Although charmed by the idea of living out a fantasy, I found myself too timid to pull it off on the social stage without a dose of courage—alcohol. Once I discovered the magical power, I used it regularly to prepare myself for socializing. We were country girls looking for thrills we never had back home.

The ambiance, seen through a sparkling glass of Beaujolais, and playing "chess" in a low-cut, black-sequined cocktail dress excited me. Flickering candlelight over the squares of the "chessboard" foreshadowed the dance on the parquet floor later. The dance was like a game for me, a series of moves toward checkmate. A daring move countered by a threat kept the tension of chess and romance moving.

I never saw myself as a drunk. A drunk is a bum. A drunk is stupid. I was different. I loved to debate, to let my intellect catch the wind of my imagination while my thoughts soared. Booze opened my mind to a library of thoughts, filling my lips with words and ideas that seduced my inflated ego. I could expound on just about anything as long as my glass was full. But my best thinking always took a turn for the worse after too many drinks.

I was having the time of my life. I didn't need help like some old drunk. Until one morning, years later. The curtain came down, the show was over.

I was a drunk!

Where does a drunk go for help? To a meeting. An AA meeting.

What is a drunk expected to do? To not drink and to keep coming to *meetings*. At first, I focused on getting to a *meeting* without taking a drink. I followed the rules. Slowly, sobriety uncovered a human being, real and without an act—but it didn't last.

Alcoholics Anonymous promises sobriety. That sounds good to someone on the bottom looking up. *The steps* to recovery began to make sense to my sobering mind. Then, out of nowhere, an insane urge drove through my mind. Like a blaring horn crashing through traffic, the urge blasted all other thoughts off the road. I wanted a drink! *I can handle just one. I'm not like the others, I can handle it. It would be OK to have just one.*

Gotcha!

Where did these lies come from? Did they come from my weak will? Was I tempted by ads on TV? Or perhaps I have an imbedded genetic message rising up out of my ancestral pool.

I believed what I was told in AA—this kind of thinking is *alcoholic thinking*. It is a symptom of the disease of alcoholism. I learned from other treatment authorities that alcoholism is a chemical imbalance, a genetically transferred disease, and that relapse confirms alcoholism as a chronic disease.

Some treatment counselors suggested I had the power within me to say no to the power of craving. The "power" to say no comes from working through the twelve-step program advocated by AA. But, contrary to popular belief, self-control through personal effort is not natural, and usually fails. Learned behavior is ambushed by the craving desires of our flesh. Our choices are made in submission to these cravings. I chose relief at any cost.

For most people, AA and rehabilitation based on self-control does not produce long-term results. People who have kept sobriety through their own efforts for a length of time are still haunted by the fear of *falling off the wagon*. At every AA *meeting*, sad and sobering confessions reveal the fear of relapse.

Where's the victory?

All programs that attempt to treat the drunk will fail as long as they approach the problem as a disease. The focus on restoring the body or re-training the mind fixes surface problems only. At the root of craving is a heart problem, not the physical organ, but that part of man which is not physical— the soul and the spirit of a person. When the heart of a person remains unchanged, we fight the battle against our flesh over and over. Deceit is found in our hearts. Spiritual treatment for addiction begins by stripping away the skin of lies we hide in.

AA calls lying *denial*. It is considered a symptom of the disease. It is a formidable wall between the dying drunk and salvation. Truth breaks down that wall. Jesus said, "I am the way, *the truth*, and the life" (John 14:6). The antidote for lying is truth.

Most recovery programs define abstinence as periods of not drinking, and recovery as a return to a stable and productive life-style over a period of time. This must include no alcoholic-drinking behavior. Current statistics on successful recovery are measured in months. These statistics are available on the Internet. The idea of total recovery from addiction is not considered by most health care providers, our court systems, or our rehabilitation centers. It is financially more profitable to treat alcoholism as a chronic disease.

A cure for man's failures in the area of indulgence, whether food, sex, or alcohol, requires a power greater than ourselves.

AA advocates a *higher power.* Why, then, are so many of those who go to the *meetings* powerless to stay sober for any length of time? The answer, I believe, is found in the Bible.

"Well," you say, "doesn't AA follow the teachings of the Bible?" It may surprise you, but AA does not endorse the Bible. They have taken great effort to show tolerance toward all faiths by defining *higher power* as whatever you want it to be.

The Bible's claim is that God is absolutely able to deliver us from our problems. It also tells us, "there is one God and one mediator between God and men, the Man Christ Jesus. . . ." (1 Tim. 2:5).

A cure is possible! Using the Bible as a textbook, I would like to show how I received complete deliverance from the bottle.

CHAPTER TWO

He drank, not as an epicure, but barbarously, with a speed and dispatch altogether American, as if he were performing a homicidal function, as if he had to kill something inside himself, a worm that would not die.
          —Baudelaire, writing about Edgar Allan Poe

This picture of drinking is all too familiar. For me, what started out as a good time ended with insanity. When I ran out of excuses for drinking, I drank until I passed out.

Killing myself? Yes! Spiritually, I felt God could not—and would not—help. Alcohol took my mind and body. Drinking problems led to health problems. My doctors, medical and psychiatric, directed me to AA. I followed their advice. They are the professionals. But, the more I regarded the diagnosis of alcoholism as a disease, the less I felt responsible for my drinking. And the crazier I got.

It's not my fault! It's a disease!

With all the help I had, I couldn't change my habit for any length of time. My psychiatrist dug into my head to find the reason for my destructive mindset. My internist gave me pills to control my agitated craziness. AA counselors told me I had inherited my problem and must come to their meetings regularly to stay sober. Their methods for helping me were all based on the theory that alcoholism is a disease.

Drunkenness is defined as self-abuse. No one can argue with that. The excuse for our "self abuse" is circumstances beyond our control. A family history, strict religious beliefs, or an abusive environment makes us alcoholic. Alcoholics are victims, they say. If our father is an alcoholic and our mother is a religious nut who beat us into living a faultless life, we have all the credentials necessary to become a full-fledged drunk. This is an extreme example, but it shows what is meant by circumstances beyond our control.

Public health taking its cue from science and medicine gears treatment toward shielding the alcoholic from further guilt and shame and not confronting the drunk with the results of his actions. "Consequences make him neurotic! They drive him to drink!" Our court system legislates against any crime committed while under the influence, but throws the drunk back into the arms of doctors and treatment centers.

If the doctors and scientists are right, alcoholism is a disease. And it's no more my fault than having the brown hair I was born with. I must have a craving response labeled "alcohol" in my system. This means some ancestor polluted my genes!

Wow! What an excuse. My arm lifts a bottle of booze to my mouth, and I guzzle it down like a brown-haired robot programmed to self-destruct.

But what if the Bible is right? What if some day God asks me why I drank so much? I can't lie to Him! Will He believe me if I tell Him, "It wasn't my fault; I have a disease"?

If I could retrain my *stinking thinking*, which drove me to drink, and change my ways, wouldn't that be enough? No! Because I would squirm and claw out from under the grinding heel of my condemning mind!

The Bible does indicate a pre-existing condition—sin. Adam's disobedience to God's command caused every generation after him to carry the stain of sin. Sin entered the gene pool of mankind. We inherit a sin nature from our parents. It is in our "skin" to sin until God removes it and we are born again.

In the Bible, James explains it like this: craving, like a fuse slipped through our senses, sparks, igniting our thoughts into flame. We choose to fan the flame or douse it. If we choose to keep the flame alive, action is pushed by what we think (James 1:13,14).

Science perceives craving as only a physical reaction. Pain caused by stress sets into motion chemicals that produce craving. Alcoholics are driven to drink to relieve the pain. Researchers seek a chemical balance to counter the craving pain. The idea is to neutralize the craving, to create bio-balance. The effect should be peace of mind.

But peace of mind can be interrupted and sabotaged by something as simple as unexpected changes in routine or the smell of brownies just out of the oven. *"I'll just taste one,"* we tell ourselves. Our bodies, like demanding two-year-olds, never have enough of a good thing; one brownie is just a tease.

We scold ourselves for overindulgence. We promise to get a hold on ourselves. Then we break our promise. Why?

How far will we go to get what we want when we want it? Scientists wanted to find out. Laboratory rats were bred to prefer alcohol to water. The rats with the yen for booze made a beeline for the bottle with the alcohol, even when the technician set up roadblocks.

But, wait a minute! Those rats don't know it's bad for them. They don't even know they are killing themselves. Human's do!

The rats were forced to crave alcohol. When a baby is force-fed alcohol through the mother's placenta, it too will crave alcohol after birth. In both cases, it was not a personal choice.

As adults however, we drink alcohol because we want to. It is our connection to God that pounds us over the head with guilt the next day after a binge. It is guilt that informs us we have transgressed the law of acceptance and reason. We are not like animals that function by instinct. We are made in the image of God. We have knowledge of right and wrong. We experience discomfort with wrong and pleasure from doing right. Unlike any other creature, we can enjoy pleasure not just in the physical but in the spiritual as well.

Human physical pleasure, like eating fresh baked bread, when enjoyed in the spiritual realm, produces gratitude and thanksgiving.

Alcohol robbed me of all pleasure and guilt. Like the writer Poe, I was trying to kill something inside me. I started out drinking like an "epicure" and finished like a "barbarian."

CHAPTER THREE

—⚬⚬⚬—

When choosing between two evils, I always like to try the one I've never tried before.   —Mae West 1892–1980

The year was 1975. Married with two children, attending college, and ready for excitement beyond the home, I became a thoroughly seventies woman. Within the college atmosphere, I found creative outlets for my stifled desires in the arts. The club-like bonding among college poets opened my eyes to a breaking loose; from lofty, inspired odes, to earthy, unrhymed philosophies in verse. Other students of poetry wrote revealing poems about their fragmented families and discontent with the established rules of conduct. Women were no longer stuck at home. Men abdicated their place as heads of their homes. Children were given more liberty to make up their own minds about right and wrong. Women tested the waters in previously forbidden areas.

The poetry in our classes centered on erotic themes. We read poets who challenged our traditional Judeo-Christian ethics and idealized hedonistic pleasure. We read and followed other writers who did what was right in their own eyes. The conventional rules of morality and responsibility were replaced on campus like last year's hemlines. Only a century before, German philosopher, Friedrich Wilhelm Nietzche proclaimed,

"God is dead." This motto prevailed instead of our national "In God We Trust."

Intoxicated with the spirit of the times, I recklessly drank in its novelty. Older than the average college student at the time, I was beguiled by their intellectual freedom from tradition. In my seventeenth-century literature class, we read John Bunyan and John Milton as if they were irrelevant and jaded by Puritan influence. But we savored their twist of words and hidden meanings. Our instructors put a new spin on these religious classics. They taught us to look at hell as a wonderful science fiction of Dante's imagination. Heaven on Earth put man at the center, where all things existed for his fulfillment and pleasure—instant gratification, not delayed. We learned that Shakespeare used words to veil his sensuous wit, making the words provocative through suggestion. This opened new ways of looking at the old traditions that confined our creative thoughts, without risking libel. The Bible offered great literature and poetry. Our professors encouraged us to read it for those reasons. Reading the Bible as literature rather than "truth" was a new concept for me.

Most colleges accepted evolution as the explanation of our beginnings and it took little imagination to connect private passions to our animal ancestors. The creative writings of the students reflected this belief. As poets, our creative impulses conceived and gave birth to poetic expressions that blatantly aroused the reader. Moral guidelines moved from the traditional center and dropped off the edge of propriety. We questioned absolutes.

A whole new life, like a kaleidoscopic web, lured me into its appealing trap. Everything I had ever learned about God and moral living paled in the glitter of desire. I looked at life through the changing patterns of the mesmerizing seventies.

I deliberately set my feet on the path that led to fun. My feet danced without hesitation toward that first addicting bite. *My life has been booring! This is fun and I'm free and happy at last! I can do whatever I want, and I don't have to answer to God!* Wanting it all, I believed the lie that there were no consequences.

I compared God to all those in authority: too strict! I flirted with other gods who would accommodate my desires. My poetry friends introduced me to Hinduism and other eastern religions that worshipped gods of pleasure.

I personally didn't believe God to be dead, but I didn't want to acknowledge Him, either. But I could not ignore God. Sunday school and church in my growing-up years stuck in my memory. The embedded knowledge of sin would not delete from my memory. A drink helped to quiet the scolding guilt inside me.

At first the alcohol loosened me up. Inhibitions that would normally prevent bawdy outbursts dissolved in a lusty toast to "the good life." Seduced into brazen confidence, I often found myself in trouble while under the influence. There is no controlling the demons of the bottle. My head danced and whirled in drunkenness until my insides spun into sudden retching.

The guilt I felt the morning after could be nicely snuffed by a little nip. More and more drinking became my whole life. I went from sipping cocktails in sequined dresses to swigging gin from an open bottle in my bathrobe. Guilt and fear of exposure set up a deadly cycle. Like a waterwheel turns as long as water fills each trough and spills into the next through pressure, so alcohol turned each day as I poured booze through my body.

Many mornings I woke with raw nerves and a touchy stomach. Waking up late in the morning after my husband and children were out of the house, my day began. I would stumble to the kitchen where a fly buzzed over dirty dishes in the sink. My slippers would stick to something spilled on the floor. I would pull the blinds; the sunlight hurt my eyes. I had stashed my bottle behind the hutch and needed a drink. As soon as the glow hit, I promised myself: *tomorrow I will quit.* A sudden shower of tears came over me as I thought of my dear children. *They deserve a good mother.* Tears flowed until I emptied out my grief and passed out.

Several hours later I would wake up. Panic would hit as I rushed around cleaning up the dishes before my husband came home for lunch.

Five years of intense drinking plunged me into a sea of inebriation that threatened to drown me. I lived in a gin bottle. The party had fizzled out like stale champagne. Booze became my god, demanding all—family, friends, and reputation. My career goals were flushed down the drain. Any conscience I had was now soaked in gin. For a quick fix, I "borrowed" money to buy a cheap bottle.

In those days I could not make decisions for my daily life. I was a prisoner shackled to a bottle of booze.

———

Everyone practicing evil hates the light and does not come to the light, lest his deeds be exposed. (John 3:20)

CHAPTER FOUR

—◦◦◦—

The only way to get rid of temptation is to yield to it.
—Oscar Wilde 1854–1900

Well, I haven't seen you in a while," she told me smugly. "I always say, when you don't come to meetings, you've unpopped the cork again!"

I gritted my teeth and stiffened my neck. I had fallen off the wagon, but I wasn't going to let her know that! *She's only guessing. I'll ignore her. Who does she think she is anyway? She's got a nerve!* I clenched my jaw and flipped my head away. *The old timers in AA are know-it-alls.*

I had been in and out of AA meetings enough times. I knew the ropes and jargon. I would come back only as a last resort. The last resort was usually precipitated by a crisis caused by my drinking. There were so many meetings in my area I could move around without seeing the same people very often. *It's a game.* (It's denial.) I thought I could fool the people who played the same games!

Alcoholics Anonymous, AA, appears spiritual. Most of the meetings take place in churches. The Lord's prayer and "Christian" words carry a religious tone.

Their reference to the higher power annoyed me. I knew who the real higher power was. It seemed ridiculous to me to call just anybody or anything, god. The true God I learned about as a child had a name: the Most High God. *Oh well, I thought, what does it matter?* Besides, my friends told me I used the word *God* too much. *Strange! I hadn't noticed.*

Bored in the meetings, my mind would wander. I looked around at the people. I sorted them out in my mind like dirty laundry. *"They" had real problems. I had a minor problem.* As I listened to their messy life stories, I judged them without ever seeing how much like them I was. I could not acknowledge my own dirty laundry hanging on my lines. It took only a few days without booze before I realized how weak-willed I really had become. But the reality of my addiction got lost in a rosy rinse of denial.

The idea that drunkenness is a sin nagged at me. I couldn't connect sickness to alcoholism without stumbling over my guilty conscience. I remembered drunks getting "saved" at church services and being delivered from booze because God had forgiven them. Here, in AA, we're always "recovering." We were told we would need these meetings for the rest of our life. I flinched at the thought of it. I knew deep down in my heart that alcoholism was a self-inflicted addiction. Still, I like getting off the hook. I could deal with a chronic disease. *Why bother God? It's a sickness, right?*

The faces around the room looked puffed, erasing smile wrinkles. Hair, stringy and limp, seemed to lengthen the droop of heavy shoulders. Many attending the meetings wore shirts advertising bars, beers, and co-naked experiences. The shirts mocked their regrettable woes. They looked like mannequins with blood-shot eyes. I knew exactly how they felt. The thought triggered flashbacks in my mind of shameful indiscretions on binges.

Two little habits made withdrawal from alcohol bearable: cigarettes and coffee! Getting a cup of coffee with the shakes to my lips took concentration. We were all alike—poor hopeless souls trying to absorb what we heard in the meetings, our brains still buzzing from the booze. Most of us sucked long drags on our cigarettes as if somehow the gases we inhaled would blow away reality. It became easier to be one of the group and accept the program than to fight it. Coffee replaced the bottle of booze. At least it was an acceptable drink to fill our mouth. Cigarettes, too, were calming. We had to have these crutches, even though smoking and boozing were usually inseparable pals.

In 1934, a man by the name of Bill W. could not control his abusive drinking. His doctor had tried everything, but nothing worked. Wanting to help Bill, his doctor developed a theory that tied alcoholism to allergies. The two men and another alcoholic devised a program they believed would give hope and help to those who battled the bottle. It was not long before an active group of men were meeting regularly to help each other stay sober. In time more groups developed. These were the beginnings of Alcoholics Anonymous.

The theory that alcoholism is a progressive disease goes back to the 1800s in America. Bill W. and his doctors perpetuated a theory passed down from another doctor's theory. In 1810, Dr. Benjamin Rush published a new concept: drunkenness as alcohol addiction. The moral influence of Christianity at the time prevailed against any further development of the idea of alcoholism as a disease. The temperance movement used some of the insights of Dr. Rush to call for total abstinence among its followers, and by 1830, over a half a million Americans practiced abstinence. Leading doctors agreed with abstention and the theory put forth by Dr. Rush. As a leading physician, educator, and signer of the Declaration of Independence, Dr. Benjamin Rush contributed greatly to an American ideal of morality.

Prohibition followed the temperance movement of intolerance toward drunkenness. The drunk was viewed not as a victim of an addiction, but a criminal, someone who broke the laws of our cities and states.

The "rediscovery of alcoholism as a disease" in the 1930s became the bed out of which our current rehabilitation philosophy arose. It was during these years when a number of physicians aggressively pursued a solution for addiction. Dr. Carl Jung and his associates were among those who were impressed with the fledging alcoholic recovery group of Bill Wilson. The idea of addiction became scientifically accepted as a person-specific addiction, without any laboratory data to prove it. Then in 1935, the birth of Alcoholics Anonymous began as an "alcohol-free" social structure that has operated as an unquestioned alcohol and drug recovery program. The medical profession accepted and redefined alcoholism as a chronic disease. Because of frequent lapses in sobriety, the categorizing of alcoholism as a chronic illness seemed justified.

In their diagnostic manual, the American Medical Association does not actually list alcoholism as a disease. However, at an AMA conference in 1987, they stated, "The American Medical Association *endorses the proposition* that drug dependencies, including alcoholism, are diseases." The doctors took a vote and decided to call alcoholism a disease without any scientific evidence.

According to the well known Hazelden Foundation, seventy-nine percent of Americans in 1999 accepted alcoholism as a disease. The survey also revealed a contradiction. While they defined alcoholism as a disease, the same respondents indicated they believed it to be a self-inflicted disease. When the survey asked about hiring someone who had completed alcohol or drug rehabilitation, forty-seven percent said they would not. Other similar questions continued to show that according to public opinion, doing drugs or abusing alcohol is a *chosen behavior* (www.hazelden.org/research/publication).

In my own experience, rehabilitation was ineffective. When AA meetings were not working, my doctor tried supplementing my treatment with a hard-core tranquilizer called Stellazine. The drug entombed me. I walked like a zombie. The shield of protection the drug provided kept me contained, but could not stop the drive to drink. The insanity of my thought-life isolated me from others. The combination of alcohol and Stellazine could have killed me. The urge to extinguish my life at this point needed no assistance from Satan. But, I couldn't even die!

All I desired was the state of numb. My tongue, like thick dough, refused to shape words. I stopped talking. Activity within my brain froze. Though catatonic, I heard the doctor say I would have to be institutionalized permanently because he could do no more for me.

"No!" I screamed. No one heard me—no one on Earth, anyway. I buried myself in a tomb under crusts of fear and denial. My eyes glazed against the outside world.

—◦◦◦—

The whole world lies under the sway of the wicked one.
(1 John 5:19)

CHAPTER FIVE

We need more than supernatural truth, we need a supernatural mind to receive it. —A. B. Simpson

God heard my cry for help. He had plans for me. They did not include vegetating in a mental institution. My mother and father took me into their home. I could not care for myself or my family. Alcohol, though a foreign substance in my body, had become a vital ingredient in my blood stream. When I didn't have it, I quaked like an aspen leaf in a storm. My muscles and nerves seized in pain. Panic held my mind hostage. At those times, I could hear a thousand sirens going off inside my body. Driven to get relief, I made choices like a starving predator, willing to commit anything to get the next drink. I swallowed my morals with a chaser of booze. As soon as I had taken enough alcohol, my body would relax. But the comfort gained from alcohol did not last long and there were no highs. In AA, this is referred to as "maintaining."

My parents love God and live by His Word. Their love and concern for me rescued me like a rope thrown to a drowning victim. But what do you do with a grown daughter who has become like a beached whale in your living room? They provided me with a sofa bed and the exclusive use of the room. They had to step around me and adjust their lives to this huge problem—*me!*

I wanted to die!

Every day my mother and father knelt before God and prayed for my deliverance. God led them to a Christian woman who worked with alcoholics as a ministry. They asked me to call her. I made an appointment to meet with her at her church. As a pastor's wife with a special burden for alcoholics, she gently asked me about myself. I felt strange talking to a pastor's wife. But she wore Levi's and lounged comfortably over the pew, making me more at ease. Her soft voice was soothing to listen to. After spending an hour talking, she hugged me. I bristled!

"I don't think your main problem is alcohol," she said.

I didn't ask her what she meant by that, but I thought, *Hey, she's all right!*

From October 1979 to January 1980, this dear woman graciously accepted my belligerence. I didn't want her around, didn't want to stop drinking, and I didn't want to live. But she kept coming back, telling me about Jesus' love for me and spoke of a new hope, a new life in Christ. She had a faith and a hope that wouldn't quit!

Bitter and angry, I refused to believe her words. *How many times have I heard all this before and what good did it do me? Who could love me now?* My face and ankles were pitted and swollen. I carried more weight than ever. I dressed in sloppy clothes, washed my hair and brushed my teeth only when forced to for an appointment. I couldn't hold a conversation and didn't care to anyway. The only expressions to cross my face revealed rage or despair. People didn't look at me, except to turn around after I had passed by. I preferred to decompose inside my skin. *Who could love me?*

Meanwhile, my parents pled with God to deliver me. I knew I caused pain in their home, but they were all I had. Worry lines plowed across their brows. Their voices trembled and strained to talk. They prayed, "Oh God, how long?"

One cold blustery day in January, I knew I had come to the end. The sub-zero, sunless day was right for dying. I stepped out on the front porch and walked down to the sidewalk. A sharp wind bit my face. I tried to cover up with a scarf but the wind playfully grabbed it. I chased after the scarf to protect my head, but now my hands hurt from the cold. Snow crunched under my thin sneakers and soon my feet were numb. *Why should I fight this weather,* I wondered. *I'll walk downtown later for a bottle.* I sat in the darkened living room, rubbing my hands. *I'm trapped! It's too blasted cold out there! I'm so disgusting. I hate myself. I can't go on like this!*

Suddenly I jumped up and ran to the room where Mother sat. *"I need help!"* Prepared for this moment by the Holy Spirit, Mother told me I needed to confess my sins to God and ask Him into my heart as Lord of my life. On my knees, I sobbed as I entered into the embrace of my loving heavenly Father. Mother advised me to give God all my bottles. She knew where they were, but insisted that I take that step of faith.

Give up my bottles? What an absurd thing to say to an alcoholic! That's crazy! Yet, her words made perfect sense to me.

The transformation, like a transfusion of life-giving blood, began, even as I took my first steps of faith toward my new heavenly Father. I went to the closet and pulled out the empties and half-empties. Holding them up I said, "Will You take this from me and give me life?"

It was over.

God washed me clean with the blood of His own dear Son, and welcomed me into the family. Death surrendered me to the true and living God who rescued me from being swallowed up in an alcoholic cesspool.

26

Carol B. Griffith

The *Most High God* is now my *Abba—daddy.*

———⟨୭୬⟩———

For you did not receive the spirit of bondage again to fear, but you received the Spirit of adoption by whom we cry out, "Abba, Father." The Spirit Himself bears witness with our spirit that we are the children of God. (Romans 8:15,16)

CHAPTER SIX

—◆◇◆—

Sin forsaken is the best evidence of sin forgiven.

—Anonymous

The doctor told his desperate patient he could do no more, "You have a chronic alcoholic brain." The patient pleaded with the well-known doctor for some reassurance of hope. The doctor said he had heard of some exceptions, but they were just an unexplained phenomena, a "vital spiritual experience."

That famous doctor was Dr. Carl Jung. He tried to reproduce in his patients a "born-again" experience through psychiatric therapy, but failed. He could not explain how a man could suddenly put away old habits and ways and take on a new life. While he had seen alcoholics healed spontaneously, he dismissed any connection to God.

Another doctor, delivered from the scourge of alcohol through a divine intervention, proclaimed, "No person is hopeless who trusts Jesus Christ to free the addict from the bondage to alcohol or drugs." This man, Dr. Addison Raws, directed the Keswick Colony of Mercy, a center dedicated to helping the despairing alcoholic by introducing him to the power of Christ over his addictions. Those who sincerely asked for help and gave God a chance to clean up their lives were cured and led successful lives following the Word of God as their source of help.

Dr. Raws saw miracles happen at his colony. He saw the supernatural acts of God alone. Here are the factors that make up a miracle according to Dr. Raws:

- Utter helplessness. (You can't do it on your own.)
- Limitless power. (Only God has this, you cannot empower yourself.)
- Faith. (Not works! Not pills! Not therapy! Not a chronic disease requiring life-long meetings.)*

The Book of Luke in the Bible records some healings. Luke was a physician and historian. References to illnesses and diagnoses show the author to be educated in the practice of medicine. Dr. Luke presented Christ as the perfect human and Savior. He argues before the religious authorities of the day for the authority and power of Jesus to forgive sins and heal all diseases. Jesus was accused of blasphemy because He called Himself God. The religious intelligentsia of the day rejected Jesus as the Son of God. They rightly associated blasphemy with the judgment of God, yet they held their religious laws and traditions as more important than knowing God, even when He stood in their midst healing the sick.

The healing and forgiving of a paralyzed man in Luke 5:17–20 points out the authority Jesus has to forgive us our sins and to heal us. In the same way, Jesus forgave me of my sins and healed me. I had come to the end of myself and knew I needed a savior. Many people prayed for me. Jesus heard and answered their prayers. Skeptical doctors, like the religious leaders of Dr. Luke's day, believed themselves to be the ultimate authorities on alcoholism. The psychiatrist and rehabilitation

---

*Addison C. Raws, *Set Free* (Hearthstone Publications, Inc. 1972. Keswick Grove, New Jersey)

counselors working with me gave up on me. The only ones who didn't give up were believers praying for me. When my doctors recommended I be committed to an institution, the believers prayed and trusted God to deliver me from my bondage.

At the appointed time, the Holy Spirit reached into my heart, sparking new life. All the pieces of my old life were arranged in preparation for my new life in Christ—the weather, my recognition of futility and need, my godly mother, waiting to guide me to Christ. I was emptied out and filled up with a new life in Christ.

Then Christ reached into the waste pool of my sin, lifting me to Himself. My shameful sins, like sewage, ran off me and over the scars on His nail-pierced hands. He exchanged my filthy rags for clean ones. For the first time in my life I *knew* the reality of God's love. He cradled me. He called me His own.

In order for us to become children of God, we must recognize there is no good in us at all, and then give up all claims on our lives. This requires a spirit of brokenness. C.I. Scofield, the editor of the *Scofield Bible,* described himself as "a drunkard, a wretch, a ruined man, who despite all his struggles, was bound in chains of his own forging." He was a man of superior ability, a lawyer in St. Louis, but he lost it all to alcohol. He came to Christ as a "little child" and gained salvation and a cure!*

Rehabilitation professionals like to refer to alcoholism as an illness. I was ill, but the illness is called "sin." The destruction of my body tissues with poison in my blood made me ill. Jesus, knowing the condition of my body and spirit, commanded a total healing. "Heal me O Lord, and I shall be healed; Save me and I shall be saved. . . ." (Jer. 17:14).

Healing is controversial. The question always comes up regarding authenticity. Is it just a dog and pony show? One

---

Moments With the Book, Gospel Series No. 40.

way to tell the real from the fake is to see what time will reveal. The day to day evidence of the change in my life has given testimony to God's intervention. Another question we might ask ourselves when trying to determine if a healing is for real is, whom does it glorify? If a showman is out to dazzle and drum up business, he will see that he gets all the credit. "God opposes the proud but gives grace to the humble" (James 4:6).

The brokenness of my spirit when I gave up my bottles for a new life in Christ came out of an unquestionable understanding—I was lost. Not just as a slave to alcohol, but in life and in death. I was a "gonner." No hope. God hears the broken heart crying, seeking. By faith (and mine was as small as a grain of mustard seed), I chose to talk to the invisible God. The words that formed on my lips came out of a heart being transformed by God. My prayer was natural: *"Daddy, help me."* I recognized my heavenly Father at last.

God makes Himself known to all people, giving every soul a chance to obtain full fellowship with Him by accepting His free gift of salvation. In Romans 1:20 we are reminded that "His invisible attributes are clearly seen, being understood by the things that are made (you and I). . . ." In this present age of grace, opportunities abound to know God.

God's infinite knowledge about us and His everlasting love for us can be understood by us as we remember why He sent Jesus to Earth in human form—all of God in a baby. He was the perfect man. He paid the ultimate price so sinners like you and me could have fellowship with His Father, as He has. He experienced all the temptations we have, yet He did not sin. You and I could never come close to that!

Biblical records as well as historical writings confirm the cruel punishment and death experienced by Jesus, King of the Jews. He was beaten, ridiculed, slapped, spat on, tortured, and crucified for our sakes. His death by suffocation was the cruelest punishment in the Roman Empire, reserved for the worst criminals. In our day we hear philosophies suggesting we are all gods or that we are capable of becoming like a god. Is this possible? Consider the cost. Look at what Jesus went through.

Think of your most painful experience. An abscessed tooth, for example. Your face is swollen and pounding with pain. Add to that the humiliation of your dentist screaming, "Don't be such a cry baby!" It's a holiday, and there is no other dentist working. The look in your teary eyes begs for help, but the dentist has no pity. Can you see yourself rising up in anguish to belt him one? The dentist sticks a metal probe into your mouth. He twists it into your hot tooth. "Does it hurt?" he snears. You ask for Novocain, but he refuses.

"No, stop!" you cry out. "I can't take any more!"

Jesus' response to His tormentors was "Forgive them, they know not what they do."

The God of the Bible is not capricious. He does not demand work for salvation. He is always the same, full of compassion. A lesser god is no higher on the ladder of virtue than you or I. How could a god we devise give us any advice? We like our gods to come down to our level of life experience. Jesus did. But He did not *sin!* Why bother with a god if he cannot improve our situation—now and later?

Jesus did not react against His attackers. He focused on the goal: salvation for all men. He finished what He came to do. Jesus, God's Son, is the extreme depth of God's love for us. Do you have someone in your life that would do all that for you? Die that you might live? Perhaps. But, Jesus rose from the grave, overcoming the power of death. He is fully qualified to give us new life. He overcame death; He is God.

God knows our beginning and our end. He is the one who knows ahead of time the best course for each of our lives. Immediate healing is not always the remedy for our problems. When we focus on trusting God, we can let go of the outcome. God is not hindered by preconceived notions as we are. We contemplate our future not knowing; God is already in the future and all-knowing. It is helpful if we turn our eyes on Him and away from our tormenting doubts and fears.

We are the work of God's hands, not our own. He molds us, shapes us, and uses every flaw to bring us to completion. On the other hand, the counsel of today is focused on ridding us of our flaws because they have no value.

Because of sin, we become broken and imperfect. But God, when we allow Him to do so, uses those imperfections to fulfill His purposes in us. Our broken parts bring suffering. How could a good God allow us to suffer? Our answer from God is sometimes difficult to understand, let alone accept. But, the more we know God the more we trust Him to make something perfect out of our messes, our hurts, our pain.

Over the past twenty-some years, God has dipped into my history pulling out the raw material of my past sins. As a Master, He knows how much filing, sanding, and buffing it will take to bring out a luster. When I share the jewels God has made from my black and damaged past, as I am doing in this book, God is showing you how He takes our trashed lives and creates a treasure.

Healing belongs to God. Modern medical cures point to man's achievements to bring relief for suffering men and women. Our bodies, however, are destined to die because sin has entered the gene pool of man through Adam. Medical intervention just delays the inevitable. God, in His mercy, endowed certain men and women with skills to help us in our sickness. When we pray for healing, we make our requests known to God. Having done that, we can rest in confidence regarding the answer. How? By praying with this attitude, the one characterized in Jesus' prayer at Gethsemane, "not my will but Thine be done." This is not an easy thing to do. Releasing our whole future into the hands of Almighty God requires a belief in the future God promised. It is like a free-fall of faith, trusting God to be there, for whatever shot He calls.

Our bodies decay and pass away. Our souls and spirits live on beyond the grave. For that reason, the most important dimension of the nature of man is the soul and spirit. Our bodies remain in the grave, but the rest of our nature lives on, awaiting that final destination, heaven or hell. God offers us eternal life in heaven through His Son, Jesus Christ.

Complete freedom from sickness, pain, and sorrow is our heavenly reward. It is our final healing into a perfect state. Revelation chapter 22 describes our healing as a pure river of the water of life. It flows from the throne of God. Jesus will bring healing to the nations. We can look forward to that day when we accept the free gift of salvation, here and now. Physical healing gained on Earth is only temporary. Our permanent healing is yet to come. We are promised a new body, once Jesus comes to rule, when all sin will be conquered.

Once I turned my life over to God, He made sure I understood my destiny. The promise in John 14 became written in my thoughts and heart. He said He would never leave me or forsake me. . . . That is the promise of a lover.

Once I had no hope. Then Jesus came. . . .

Looking up with brokenness, my eyes saw God. I knew He had the answer to all my needs. My numbed tongue began to sing— break out into joyous laughter—exalting God. Praise naturally bubbled from my heart to my lips. My eyes cupped the overflow of glad tears.

The curtains of sin drawn back, my eyes were as windows opened for the first time. Understanding burst over my mind like the morning sun. The Word of Life, Jesus, began writing my new life. The dew-sprinkled grass of that morning sparkled like emeralds. Pushing my bare feet through the damp grass seemed baptismal.

Drawing in a deep breath, I could almost taste the fresh aroma in the blue sky. The warble of a robin struck chords in my heart, tapping fountains of joy. I sang, "I am loved, I am loved!" What can match the knowledge of the love of God in my heart? The robin exalts his Creator, and now I know why.

God has blessed us with our first grandson. Fresh from his mother's womb, his skin felt like pure silk, so delicate to touch. Yet, the skin God wrapped him in would last a lifetime. I wondered how many bruises this fragile life would take.

When I first began walking with God in sobriety, I too felt fragile. God wrapped me, however, in skin that would endure the shifting circumstances of my life. I knew I would not leave my skin until He was finished with it!

We marveled how the baby quieted when he heard his parents speak. Hours old, he would turn his head in the direction of their voices. This intimate knowledge of who he belonged to is so like the knowledge I had as God revealed Himself to me, calling me by name.

Our baby grandson loves to be rolled up like a little sausage. He seems to feel secure wrapped up in a swaddling blanket. The blanket keeps him from flailing his arms and legs, giving him touchable boundaries.

We too need to know our limits and our position in Christ. God, our loving Father, swaddles us in His loving protection from unseen dangers. Peace is in His presence. We can call on Him any time of the day or night. He is always listening.

My son and his wife are always listening for little whimpers and movements from the baby. They sleep with one ear turned on and are ready in an instant to meet the little one's needs. Our heavenly Father responds to His children even before they cry!

God did for me what I could not do for myself. The best medicine had to offer could not save me from the stranglehold of booze. I could not control my cravings. Sobriety through the twelve steps was not effective. My sins were killing me. The world did not see my sin as the problem; it failed to bring about any permanent change. I could have died physically from alcohol, but my sins would have sentenced me to an eternity in hell!

———◦◦◦———

To those who sit in the prison house . . . I am the Lord, that is My name; and My glory I will not give to another, Nor my praise to carved images, Behold the former things have come to pass. And new things I declare . . . Sing to the Lord a new song. (Isaiah 42:7–10)

CHAPTER SEVEN

—ᴄᴠᴠ—

When you educate a man in the mind and not morals, you educate a menace to society.

—Franklin D. Roosevelt

A s Americans we have personal freedom. Yet, you and I know what it is like to be bound in the prison of alcohol. We are free in every way, except from our self-imposed prisons. We put ourselves in bondage, then refuse a pardon and freedom when offered by God.

Most treatment programs refuse to accept God's pardon and forgiveness. It is the belief in God they consider the stumbling block. Even worse, we give our doctors and advisors permission to keep us locked up in addiction by accepting their belief that we will always be alcoholic. We therefore learn that God does not heal that disease. Our beliefs are either for us or against us. These rehabilitation programs teach us to choose what and whom we will believe in, unless it is God's way.

Teaching our minds to accept alcoholism as a disease is easy to do. Our teachers are qualified and knowledgeable about the disease. God teaches us to avoid drunkenness and all kinds of evil behavior associated with intoxication. God uses the "S" word to describe our condition. He sets a moral boundary for drinking. While scripture does not use the word *addiction*, it is inferred in the Ten Commandments as another god. Alcohol demands total submission, above all else, including God and family.

We "believe" the power of alcohol over us. It's real. That is the definition of belief! It is real and true. Does it make us feel any better to "believe" this fact? No. As a matter of fact, it is so uncomfortable to admit our powerlessness to addictive substance that we lie about it. The lie is the language of Satan. He fills our mind with compelling half-truths. We are persuaded by his arguments. Only the power of God's truth can oppose Satan's delusions.

The voice that tickles our ears with sweet temptations is not an "addictive voice," but the language of Satan. Scripture tells us that we do not fight against "flesh and blood, but against the powers of this dark world . . . spiritual forces of evil" (Eph. 6:12).

According to some behavior modification theories, belief systems are the direct cause of consequences (guilt and shame) for our drinking. Faith-based beliefs are considered by most rehabilitation professionals as changeable and short-lived, like emotions.

It is my belief that alcoholism is not a disease but an act of sin, a choice. Craving brings suffering. We can either take a drink and delay our pain, or we can tough it out until the craving subsides. Suffering is a fact of life. It is the hard cold *reality* of the consequences of sin. When we face up to ourselves, the pain of remorse and guilt bites us. We flinch. The truth knocks us to the ground.

Where can I hide from myself—from God? Then, suddenly, truth flashes, splashing light on you. All the confusion and misery you have worn drops off into darkness. All you see is the One in the light. "God?" your spirit asks.

Our hearts have a deep longing, an "inescapable stress," reaching out for a connection to the very One who made us. As

God's creation, we look for purpose and meaning in our daily lives. And it's as uncomplicated as a simple prayer lifted from a sincere heart.

This is a reality, the truth, and a belief. This belief sets us free. It is not short-lived, but eternal. It is not an emotional reaction, but an actual transaction between God and us, maintained by His power.

———

Let us strip off and throw aside every encumbrance (unnecessary weight) and that sin which so readily and cleverly clings to and entangles us . . . looking to Jesus Who is the Leader and the source of our faith . . . (Hebrews 12:1, 2 AMP)

CHAPTER EIGHT

White washing the pump doesn't make the water pure.
—D. L. Moody

Once I had experienced a conversion, I needed to learn how to walk by faith. Just as a baby takes incremental steps, so is the progression of our walk with Christ. We allow God to take control of our whole being—our heart, our thoughts, and our attitudes. Alcohol rots our thinking and our attitude stinks like bad breath. When our hearts have been made clean through conversion, our minds and attitudes must be surrendered to God daily, with His help. God will shape our attitudes as we allow Him to; He restores our minds, brings a luster to our thoughts and wipes out the smudge of confusion (1 Cor. 14:33).

My family did not trust me, though they were glad to have me back in their lives. Alcohol had taken me from them, now God was restoring our family, and me. I couldn't blame them for not trusting me. After all I had broken promises and lied to them while drinking. God clothed me with grace and understanding. He help me to live "in truth" by not retreating into self-pity when they questioned me. Sometimes, at the table, the kids would take my glass and sneak a sip. "Just checking!" they'd say when I caught them. I knew I had to win back their trust. This meant I had to become totally honest.

Telling the truth was not an easy thing for me to do. After all I had become skilled at deception. It took little trials for me to trust truth! I had to daily commit to being honest and ask God for His help—especially when I feared consequences.

One day I backed the car right into the side of the garage. I knew my husband would think I had been drinking again. *Oh God, please give me courage!* My heart seemed to pound right through my chest, but I confessed.

My honesty was rewarded with little signs of trust, instead of suspicions.

Our wholeness and strength lies in being with God. This takes discipline, something I had not taken up in a long time! I needed to ask the Lord to help me take time out each day to pray, meditate on His Word, and to praise Him.

After God had healed me from alcohol, I continued to go to AA meetings. Every time I would say in a meeting, "God is my higher power," people got nervous. Even though I felt inexperienced and vulnerable with the old-timers in AA, I knew I could not deny what had happened to me. If I referred to myself as just a "recovering" alcoholic, I would be lying. It was not long before I stood on the truth of my healing by God and trusted Him alone to keep me. AA wanted me to keep coming back to meetings. I yearned to live victoriously, leaving behind the old ways. I had become a new person in Christ and I wanted to enjoy my freedom.

And I am sure that God who began the good work in you will keep right on helping you grow in grace until his task within you is finally finished on that day when Jesus Christ returns. (Phil. 1:6 TLB)

If I had denied the power of Jesus Christ over the sin and destruction in my life, I would need to trust in my own resources. I could try to stick to a program, but the power to keep it working was not in me. I realized I was powerless without God.

Accountability to another person helped to bolster my commitment to walking with God. I chose a reliable friend, who understood the necessity of seeking God's will for my daily life. She had never had an alcohol problem, but she had the best wisdom in the world at her fingertips—the Bible and its Author. I had to be willing to be open and honest with my friend, whether it was good or bad. Programs using the twelve steps of AA suggest a sponsor from within the program to keep a person straight. But this draws its wisdom from man. As a new Christian, freed from alcohol, I needed God's wisdom— step-by-step instructions in the Bible. Choosing a helper who used God's Word as the authority, and who included God in all matters, brought results.

It would seem foolish in the eyes of this world's professionals to trust an ex-alcoholic's word or the untrained counsel (alcoholic counselor) of other Christians. "For what man knows the things of a man except the spirit of the man which is in him? Even so no one knows the things of God except the Spirit of God . . . (Christians) teach in words not of man's wisdom but which the Holy Spirit teaches" (1 Cor. 2:11,13).

As I read through different Bible promises, I savored the taste, like a fresh-picked orange. I knew it was good for me, and the flavor was so delicious. I learned to memorize favorite verses and tuck them in my heart. Later, I could bring them back from memory and enjoy the deliciousness all over again. God's word is like honey. It nourishes us and protects against the infection of sin. I even personalized some of the verses in the Bible by writing my name into the phrase. For example, "God so loved *Carol* that He gave His only begotten Son. . . ." (see John 3:16). Every time I would see my name written in

God's Word, it reminded me that my relationship to God was very personal. The overwhelming transformation of my life provided visible proof to me, and to others. He doesn't leave us without recognizable evidence of His work of grace in our lives. He has given me twenty-one years of sobriety as a record of fact. It is my personal history, written by the hand of God. I often meet people who say, "You don't act like an alcoholic!" These people give witness to the redeeming work of grace by God in me.

I am not an alcoholic. I used to be one. You can have a new life, too. Just ask God. He's waiting for you!

———✿✿✿———

Look! I have been standing at the door (of your heart) and I am constantly knocking. If (your name) hears me calling him and opens the door, I will come in and fellowship with (your name). (See Revelation 3:20 TLB)

HEALING FOR YOUR HEARTACHE

Rx: Capsules of truth to be taken daily for good spiritual health!

Promise of salvation: John 3:16
Promise of forgiveness: 1 John 1:9
Promise of victory over temptation: 1 Corinthians 10:13
Promise of His presence: Hebrews 13:5
Promise of victory through God's Word: Psalm 119:11
Promise that He hears us: 1 John 5:14,15

BIBLIOGRAPHY

—◦◦◦—

Alcoholics Anonymous World Services, Inc. *Alcoholics Anonymous*. 3rd ed. Alcoholics Anonymous World Services, Inc. New York City: 1976.

Alcoholics Anonymous World Services, Inc. *Alcoholics Anonymous Comes of Age: A Brief History of AA*. Alcoholics Anonymous World Services, Inc. New York City: 1976.

Almy, Gary, and Carol Tharp Almy, with Jerry Jenkins. *Addicted to Recovery*. Eugene, Oregon: Harvest House, 1994.

Anderson, Neil T. *The Bondage Breaker*. Eugene, Oregon: Harvest House Publishers, 1990.

Ankerberg, John, and John Weldon. *The Facts on Self-Esteem, Psychology, and the Recovery Movement*. Eugene, Oregon: Harvest House Publishers, 1995.

"Call it Sin!" *Daily Bread*. RBC Ministries. (July 18, 1998).

"Countering the Cults." *RBC Discovery*. RBC Ministries. (July 1980).

Dunn, Jerry, with Bernard Palmer. *God is for the Alcoholic*. Chicago: Moody Press, 1965, 1986.

Ellis, Albert, and Emmett Velten, *Rational Steps To Quitting Alcohol: When AA Doesn't Work for You*. Fort Less, New Jersey: Barricade Books Inc., 1992.

Freeman, Hobart. *"Every Wind of Doctrine."* Faith Ministries Publicatons, 1974.

Goodwin, Dr. Donald W. *Alcoholism, the Facts*. 3rd ed. Oxford University Press, 1995.

Hester, Reid K., and William R. Miller. *Handbook of Alcoholism: Treatment Approaches, Effective Alternatives*. 2nd ed. Albuquerque, NM. University of New Mexico, 1995.

Hunt, Dave. "God as You Conceive Him/Her/It to Be." *The Berean Call*. Bend, Oregon. (August 1997).

Jellinek, E.M. "Disease Concept of Alcoholism." Rutgers Center of Alcohol Studies, 1960, New Brunswick, NJ.

"Lessons From Rock Bottom." *Christianity Today.* vol. 44, no. 8 (July 10, 2000, p. 72).

McCrady, Barbara S., and Sadi Irvine Delaney. *Self-Help Groups,* Handbook on Alcoholism Treat Approaches: Effective Alternatives, Pergamon Press, 1989, Chapter 10.

Raws, Addison C. *Set Free: Living Proof That No Alcoholic Needs to Despair.* Williamsport, PA: Hearthstone Publications, Inc., 1972.

Ruden, Ronald A., M.D., Ph.D., with Marcia Byalick. *The Craving Brain.* 2nd ed. Perennial, An Imprint of Harper Collins Publishers, New York, New York: Harper Collins Publishers, 2000.

"Set Free, Cured!" Dr. C.I. Scofield's *Deliverance.* Telling the Truth in Type and Tape Ministries, Gospel Series No. 40, Bedford, PA.

The Twelve Steps for Christians. *Friends in Recovery.* Rev. ed. Curtis, WA: RPI Publishing, Inc. 1988, 1994.

Trimpley, Jack. *Rational Recovery, The Revolutionary Alternative to Alcoholics Anonymous: The New Cure for Substance Addiction.* New York, New York: Pocket Books, 1996.

Watkins, William D. *The New Absolutes: How They Are Being Imposed on Us, How They Are Eroding Our Moral Landscape.* Minneapolis, Minnesota: Bethany House Publishers, 1996.

Web Sites:

http://skepdic.com (The Skeptics Dictionary)

NIAAAHomePage (National Institute Alcohol Abuse and Alcoholism-Press Releases)

www.alcoholics-anonymous.org

www.austria-tourism.at/personen/freud/freud1_e.html

www/christianrecovery.com/library

www.foxnews.com, Oreilly Factor.

www.haverford.edu/psych/ddavis/jungfreu.html

www.hazelden.org/research/publication

www.rational.org/recovery/

REVIEW OF SOME COMPETITIVE TITLES

—⌘—

Recovery through science or the Bible

The secular market on self-help for addiction is based on the doctrine set forth by AA. They give man an excuse for his bad behavior. The methodology varies, but the burden for recovery is founded on man's ability to follow logic, to control his will, and to redeem himself.

Jack Trimpley in *Rational Recovery* recommends that the alcoholic just say no to alcohol. He suggests that man can overcome his addictions by exercising his mind over the matter. An "addictive voice" tells us we need a drink, according to Trimpley. He has developed a program to equip the drunk with the ability to say no to the addictive voice. Mr. Trimpley does not believe AA is effective, and, though he does not see alcoholism as an incurable disease, he does not believe it to be a sin.

The Craving Brain by Ronald Ruden sees the alcoholic as having inherited survival needs from an "old brain." He follows the theory of evolution to show how the message, "I need a drink or I'll die," is directly related to a primitive instinct. Dr. Ruden shows how he would re-train the brain to not crave alcohol.

The Twelve Steps for Christians, put out by Overcomers Outreach by RPI Publishing, takes the format and words from the twelve steps of AA and "Christianizes" them. This approach seems to deny that God can and will transform us. When we focus on our problems and ourselves, we take our eyes off God and what He can do. Using the twelve steps as a recovery tool can hinder the maturity of new life in Christ by never moving beyond the problem to an abundant life.

When I came across Jerry Dunn's book, *God is for the Alcoholic,* I finally found a kindred spirit. His book gives many examples of the transformed alcoholic's life. It is practical, it is down to earth, and it clearly puts God and not a program in the driver's seat.

There are some current booklets out that give a compelling argument for the false teaching of these recovery movements and how they have duped Christians. John Ankerberg's booklet, *The Facts on Self-Esteem,* and Dave Hunt's newsletter, The Berean Call, reveals the dangers of the "God as you conceive Him to be" concept of AA. This New Age teaching denies God as the only true God.

Addicted to Recovery, by Gary and Carol Almy with Jerry Jenkins, is a handbook on how the psychotherapeutic programs of today keep us in bondage. They coddle and prevent the sinner from claiming his inheritance and freedom in Christ.

The bibliography I presented in the beginning contains the resources I used. I believe there is a place for my viewpoint on the shelves of bookstores. My story not only shows how God can and does deliver us from *all* our diseases, but it reveals how dangerous and misleading the prevailing treatment programs are. It also blows the myth of AA and the disease concept off its secure moorings in the health care world.

—Carol B. Griffith

This book is meant to honor God,
and for His use
to rescue
the dying.

My thanks to those saints who encouraged,
who prayed,
who loved me,
who helped me write this book.

—◦◦◦—

To order additional copies of

ALCOHOLIC
BY CHOICE

Have your credit card ready and call
Toll free: (877) 421-READ (7323)

or order online at
www.winepresspub.com

or send $8.00* each plus $4.95 S&H** to

WinePress Publishing
PO Box 428
Enumclaw, WA 98022

*WA residents, add 8.4% sales tax
**add $1.50 S&H for each additional book ordered

To contact author:
E-mail: drinknomore1@juno.com
or visit her web site at
www.carolbgriffith.com